Facebook Marketing

*Learn how you can grow any Facebook page to 1
million likes in the first 6 months.*

Pamela Russell

Introduction

Congratulations on purchasing this book and taking the initiative to further your understanding of Instagram, one of today's most popular social media platforms.

Congratulations on purchasing this book and taking the initiative to further your understanding of Facebook, today's most popular social media platform.

With the revolutionary societal changes brought by *globalization* and *digitalization*, the way in which we communicate with one another has changed forever. At the click of a button, we have access to almost everyone in the world—with this phenomenon come infinite opportunities. From making friends anywhere in the world, to acquiring new customers for your developing business, we have never been connected so well.

Facebook is the most widespread social media platform today; with over **1.9 billion monthly active users** this platform boasts a truly global reach. I have been involved in the marketing industry for a long time, from television ads to infomercials I always loved my job. Recently, I have grasped the opportunities offered by the power of social media to expand my reach to a global audience. Never before have I felt so powerful and well connected to my audience.

Throughout my career I have grown eight Facebook pages to over **1 million likes** – that's a massive audience you are able to interact with every day, for FREE.

In this book I will explain key digital marketing strategies I have developed to quickly capture and engage a large audience and hence grow any Facebook page massively. From launching effective ad campaigns to outsourcing and building a monetary income from your page, this book will teach everything you need to **grow a Facebook page to 1 million likes in the first 6 months!**

REE GUIDE - How You can Earn
IONEY from your Facebook Page.

Available at:
www.bit.ly/facebookpageincome

Table of contents

Chapter 1- Introduction to Facebook Marketing

Over the past decades our society has been completely reshaped and overturned by the rising global phenomenon of *digitalization*. With the rapidly decreasing costs of high speed broadband and consumer electronics, digital media now impacts the majority of our daily lives. From sharing stories with our best friends to advertising new brands by young entrepreneurs, digitalization has revolutionized the way we communicate with one another. Social Media platforms are the drivers of this revolution, such platforms allow us to share writing, images and videos to anyone anywhere in the world *instantly*.

Facebook is the most successful and popular social network today. With **1.9 billion** monthly active users, this platform has a truly global reach. To the common user Facebook represents the perfect way to keep in touch with friends, but to the cunning mind of any entrepreneur this massive database of users represents *opportunity*.

Indeed Facebook is considered the cheapest, most effective platform for advertisement in today's world. Gary Vaynerchuck, marketing genius creator of Vaynermedia, recommends that brands should only advertise using Facebook or during the Superbowl.

The power of Facebook marketing relies on three main strengths: (1) Global Reach (2) Targeted Advertising (3) Instantaneous and Detailed Feedback. This book will teach you exactly how to use these 3 key strengths to acquire and engage an audience of millions of users quickly and effectively.

Chapter 2 – Blueprint to 100,000 Page Likes

This is the exact same strategy that I have used to grow many Facebook pages to 100,000 likes within 3 months of their creation. An initial investment of about 50$ to dramatically accelerate the initial growth of the page is required, beyond that I recommend only organic growth until the target is met.

Provided the steps below are followed with rigor and the marketing strategies presented later in this book are thoroughly applied, you will successfully grow any Facebook page to over 100,000 likes.

Post in Cato Page

Step 1- Choose & refine your page theme.

The page should only contain content that matches your page theme, do not go off topic (see chapter 5 for more information of page themes). You must find an appropriate trade-off between maintaining a large target audience and refining your niche to perfectly represent and fulfil market demands.

Step 2 – Define your target customer and determine the market demands

In order to post content that engages and attracts a wide audience, you must understand who it is aimed at and what they are looking for – in marketing terminology these are the target audience and market demands. Develop a profile (age, hobbies, activates, gender …) of your target audience and then explore what they are looking for (i.e. market demand and value proposition). You must appreciate what your audience needs, so you can create content that meets their demand—that is how you achieve user engagement and rapid growth *(see chapters 6&7 for more detail)*.

It is important to develop a first insight into your target audience before starting the page. As your page scales and gains momentum, it will attract a wider audience. To maximize the growth of your page you must always understand the demographics of the users you are targeting. Facebook provides the perfect tools to achieve this: **Facebook Analytics** (see chapter 10) and testing the response to **Facebook Advertisement** (see chapter 9).

The insights gained into your target audience using these tools can apply to any social media platform.

Step 3 – create page and post initial content

You are now ready to create a Facebook page and begin with your first posts. First, you must fill in all the page information and add high-quality background/profile pictures for your page (if you need logo/graphic designs use fiverr.com).

Afterwards, you should create 5-10 high quality post that fit the theme of your page/theme strategy *(see chapter 5)*. Although the first posts may not be the best quality you will ever produce, they should provide your page an initial sense of direction, style and recognisability. They should summarise everything your page wants to be and will be to any new visitor.

Step 4 – Launch your first Marketing Campaign to 10,000 likes (maximum 50$)

Once you have defined your page theme, content strategy and have created 5-10 posts that represent your page, it is time to launch your first ad campaign!

In chapter 9 I show you exactly how I gained 5,000 likes for $15. The marketing campaign I present is perfectly repeatable, if you launch the same campaign you will experience similar results. I regularly use it for new pages and I consistently experience a similar level of success. *launch same campaign*

Use this campaign to gain your first 10,000 likes for a maximum of $50. Note these likes are not from your target audience and they will not improve user engagement. The purpose of this campaign is to gain a high amount of likes rapidly and provide future visitors the social proof needed to engage in your content. Remember, it is difficult to attract new users when your page has 13 likes; it is a lot easier when your page has 13,000 likes. *more likes attract more users*

After this point, you should let your page grow mostly ORGANICALLY to 100,000 likes. You are free to launch any further campaigns if you have the budget, but these should be "boost your post" campaigns targeting user engagement/reach (See chapter 3).

Step 5 – find & acquire high engagement users

High engagement users are those who tend to be extremely active on Facebook. They comment on posts, tag their friends, like every picture. Acquiring as many of these users as possible is the key to a rapidly increasing page value, visibility, exposure and growth. The strategy below describes how to find & attract these users:

i. Go on Facebook pages similar to yours and follow hashtags that match your page theme. *#like mine?*

ii. Look in the comment section. Search for the users who post many comments/tag their friends.

iii. Send them an invite to your page. Like their comments and reply with something positive and supportive, for instance "great post, I love [shared page theme]" or "impressive page, your content always catches my eye". *Compliment them*

iv. These users will receive a notification stating you liked/commented/invited them; chances are they will glance back at your page. This is the precious moment where you must capture their attention, fill their market needs and thus acquire a new audience member! Do not be surprised if you have a low retention rate at first, people are less inclined to follow small. As your profile increases in size, you refine your theme and you perfect your content the conversion rate will increase also.

This entire process can be outsourced (see chapter 12) or automated using bots (see chapter 4), at very reasonable costs.

Step 6 - Regular, high frequency posting pattern

Posting once a day or less works well for small pages, but as your following increases your posting frequency must increase also. Pages with more than 50,000 likes should post at least twice a day for maximum user engagement and growth. If you have a well-defined content strategy and style templates as described in chapter 11, you can **outsource** some of your posts for a very low-cost (see chapter 12)

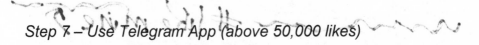

Step 7 – Use Telegram App (above 50,000 likes)

This is a key, little known secret to rapid social media growth. Most successful and large pages use it. In fact, it is almost necessary to organically grow beyond 50,000 likes. Within Telegram, there are private groups of very popular pages with up to millions of likes. When a member of the group has a new post, all group members will immediately like it and comment (the process is automatic). When a large number of very high ranking, famous pages like a single post in a short amount of time, you will gain a high-amount of visibility and peak engagement. If the post attracted this number of famous, popular profiles the post must be very valuable. This is how Facebook posts go VIRAL!

How do you join a Telegram group? Contact large pages that share similar interests and ask if you can join their telegram account. Do not be afraid to contact very large accounts directly. They benefit from having you in their groups because they will receive additional likes and comments, even if your following is a bit smaller.

Step 8 – Collaborations or Shoutout-4-shoutout (pages of similar size)

As you start developing a large following (50,000 likes is the minimum), you can contact pages of a similar size asking to organize a collaboration, also known as shoutout-4-shoutout.

Once agreed with another page, the routine procedure is sharing one of their posts for a limited time period (15 minutes - 1 hour) with a link to their Facebook page in the description, while they do the same. This cross promotion strategy is extremely useful in expanding the user engagement and reach of both pages quickly. Again, do not hesitate contacting many pages and accounts for this type of promotion, it benefits both users! Finding, contacting and negotiating with numerous pages every day requires a lot of work, but is a key strategy towards expanding your business rapidly and effectively. Again, this is a perfect opportunity for **outsourcing potential** (see chapter 12). When I am pushing for maximum page growth, I make sure my pages are doing at least 25 s-4-s every day!

Chapter 3 – Blueprint to 1 Million Page Likes

The eight steps presented above should be enough to reach 100,000 likes, provided you devote enough time, effort and have correctly applied all the marketing advice in this book. Beyond 100k likes, your approach to further growth should be quite different.

At 100,000 likes your page should be large enough to have established revenue streams that can finance outsourcing the day-to-day maintenance of your page and your marketing campaigns. If you have not established any revenue streams from your page yet, you should do that RIGHT NOW! See chapter 12 to learn more. Reaching 1 million likes is difficult and it will require a lot of work. These are the three key strategies you must follow to achieve the goal:

Strategy #1 – "Boosting your post" Facebook ads – increase Engagement & Reach

If you followed the strategy presented in this book, you only employed Facebook Ads to gain your first 10,000 likes; the remaining 90,000 likes have been purely organic. To reach the next milestone of 1 million likes, you should establish a rigid advertising strategy. I am a strong believer that a page should support itself, for this reason I recommend spending only what you earn directly from the page.

Launch regular "Boost Your Post" ad campaigns to maximize growth towards 1 million likes. After each campaign you should assess the results, adapt and improve. See chapter 9 to learn how you can launch a successful ad campaign targeting user engagement.

Strategy #2 - Buy shoutouts from very large pages

Very large Facebook pages will typically sell Shoutouts to other pages with a similar theme, send these pages a direct message and make an offer. This process can often be expensive, but shoutouts from a page with millions of followers can have a very drastic impact. I have grown a Facebook page from 100k to 400k with a single shoutout from a page with 6 Million followers. The price for this was $7,000 but the impact it had on the growth of the page was clearly immense. I was able to finance this investment with the profits earned from my other social media pages. Once your page becomes large enough, you can also sell shoutouts to earn a clearly significant income.

Strategy #3 – FOCUS on collaborating with larger pages

Of course - as your page grows in audience and engagement - you can start approaching larger pages for collaboration, which in turn give you a higher growth. When I want a page to grow quickly I aim for 25 shoutouts a day. This is an extreme amount of work, but it can be automated using bots or outsourced easily at a very low-budget (see chapter 12 for detailed information on effective outsourcing).

Chapter 4 – Fundamental Concepts & Resources for Digital Marketing

In this chapter I aim to cover the fundamental concepts of digital marketing. An understanding of these principles is required to fully grasp the marketing strategies and tactics presented later in this guide. A number of useful resources to help you enter the world of digital marketing are also provided, for instance how you can get a unique company logo design for as little as $5.

Target Audience

In the world of digital marketing, a solid understanding of the target audience is indeed required for success. Your target audience is the demographic of people most likely to be interested in your profile, this includes where they live, their age range, their gender distribution, and their daily habits. Understanding these key characterises is necessary to tailor your content to their interests/needs/habits, thus maximizing engagement and growth.

Value Proposition

These are the characteristics, features and aspects that make a page or product attractive to an audience. You should strive to answer the question **"why would my target audience follow this page?"** Although the followers may be unaware of a profile's value proposition, the admin must have a complete appreciation of it if he wants to reach success. If the page admin wishes to widen his target audience, he must broaden the value proposition to match the demands of new users.

10

What exactly does a value proposition consist of? The page below has **1.8 Million** Likes, let's try to analyse its value proposition:

Case Study Analysis: simple value proposition of "Grumpy Cat Memes"

1. Users value this page because it makes them laugh
2. Users value this page because it contains cute cats with unrealistic expressions
3. Users value this page because it conveys unlikely and relatable messages through the personification of a cat

Post Reach

The reach of a post represents the amount of people that have seen the post. These users did not necessarily interact with the post by commenting or liking it, merely how many users the post reached. This metric is very useful when calculating conversion rates – what fraction of users who viewed this post proceeded to like my page?

Importance of user engagement

Remember the profitability of any social media page is determined by user engagement. Engagement is what shows its true following and user commitment to the page. Similarly the value of many tech companies is determined by daily active users or monthly active users, not registered users. Engagement is widely recognized as a universal metric for brand value, than simple page likes. For this reason, the number of likes, on average, can be better representative of value than the amount of followers a page has.

High engagement users

These users are the key to increasing user engagement, profitability and the following of your page. High engagement users are characterised for being very extremely active on Facebook: they like many posts, they tag their friends, they send links and they post lots of comments. Acquiring this key portion of your target audience is what will give your Facebook page immense visibility, engagement and a rapid growth. A key strategy to target and acquire high engagement followers is explained in later chapters.

Bots

A key part of your page growth is commenting and liking on every post coming from similar pages and similar hashtags. Searching and posting 500 comments a day-believe me-requires a lot of time! To speed up the process, Facebook bots have been developed to automatically do this for you. For a very small investment sum bots can search pages, search hashtags, post comments and like on your behalf. An example of a bot with this capability is *followliker*, but there are many out there. Make sure you do your search into all available bots, learn their capabilities and finally choose the one best suited to your social media requirements.

Useful Resources

Bitly.com – Track how many times a URL is clicked over time. This resource is free and very easy to understand.

Fiverr.com – Here you can get a wide amount of jobs done for just $5. I recommend using it for one-off tasks. Typical things it can be used for: design brand logos, graphic design, writing item descriptions, writing biographies, etc…

Upwork.com – This website is perfect to hire Freelancers for extended work projects. You can advertise job posts, applications and –for important jobs – I recommend arranging Skype interviews. You can hire anyone from Indian customer service employee in India to an MBA graduate working for 120$/hr

Wix.com – Free resource to create & publish your own website. For simple websites, it is easy and quick to use.

Wordpress.com – Free to create a website, but you must pay for hosting fees and domain. This framework is used to build large and complicated sites, but takes time to learn how to do so efficiently.

Pixabay.com – This is my favourite website for copyright-free images. It is important to use images without copyright in all of your entrepreneurial activities!

Chapter 5 – Choose & refine your page theme

Any successful Facebook page must be centred on a single, well-defined theme. Whether fitness, flowers, cars, a brand or a person's life— your page must contain content only relating to this theme. Write down your page theme using pen and paper in a couple of words maximum, read it and see if it matches your vision for the page. By writing it down, the page theme becomes a final target set within your mind. When choosing a page theme you should follow these two criteria if your goal is to build a large following.

Criteria #1— you must be knowledgeable and passionate about this theme. During the early stages of your page you will have to do extensive amounts of market analysis, assessing the competitors and search for *that little something* that makes your page unique. You will have to dedicate a lot of time and effort to this task, if it covers something you love it will be far simpler and more enjoyable.

Criteria #2—the theme must appeal to a large number of people if you want to reach a millions of users. You might have a very strong passion for Japanese ants, but I am afraid you might be one of very few people interested in the subject… **your target audience is simply too small**. A page can engage millions of users only if millions of people are interested in its message (value proposition). A great suggestion is to start on a broader theme, test out different markets and direct your page where you encounter the most positive user feedback.

After you have refined your theme to a sufficiently small target audience and your value proposition perfectly matches the market needs, you will acquire very loyal and highly engaged users following your Facebook page. **These users will drive**

the growth of your page. Once you have acquired all/most of users in this niche you can broaden your content and value proposition to incorporate a wider audience. This is how you build market domination over social media.

Example strategy

An example of an initial broad theme is **luxury travel**. After evaluating initial feedback, you may choose to test out narrower themes of private jet chartering, white-sand Caribbean beaches and yacht sailing. After detailed feedback evaluation, you might see yacht sailing receives highest user engagement, so that is what you focus your page on (you might want to refine your theme page further i.e. catamaran/race boats…, but for the sake of this example it is not necessary). Now, that your page is highly focused to a specific niche, you can produce content that perfectly meets the wishes of yacht sailing-enthusiasts. You will build and acquire very high-engagement users who love your content and have a high page-loyalty. After capturing the majority of the audience in your niche (i.e. your page is no longer growing) you can expand the breadth of your page to expand your target audience and hence acquire new customers. You will maintain most of the high-engagement followers acquired due their emotional investment in your page, but you are now able to approach an entirely new target audience. As you begin to dominate more and more niches, you decide to broaden your page again to target much wider markets and audiences.

This is the key to building a massive following: refine your page to a specific niche (refined theme) until you dominate that market, then target another niche and dominate it, so forth.

Chapter 6 – Understand your target Audience

As described earlier, a thorough and exhaustive understanding of your target audience is required to produce engaging content. Your aim is to engage your users, make them love your content and the brand it represents. As an online marketer (yes, that is what you are now) your only objective is to make your audience fall in love with your brand. They must love it to the point that they will recommend it to everyone they know, they will share it with all their friends and it is the one they will choose over your competitors every single time.

So, how do you discover the ins and outs of your target audience? Before we begin, you must keep in mind the two essential requirements of your audience:

Requirement #1 – Your Audience must have an Interest in the theme/subject of your page

Requirement #2 – *Your Audience must be active on Facebook*

Now you can begin identifying your audience. These are people who must **fit the two requirements above**. The five questions below will help you gain a better picture and understanding. Think them over carefully and thoroughly brainstorm to visualize who your page and content is aimed at. You are trying to get into the brain of your target audience, understand everything about them. This will help you optimize and shape your content to suit the needs of your users, thus engaging them.

Q1 – How old are they? What is their age range? Are they teenagers?

Q2 – Where do they live? Are there any language barriers? Time differences?

Q3 – Are they Men or Women?

Q4 – How to they spend their day? Are they Students? Are they young workers? Do they have families? What are their priorities?

Q5 – What do they use social media for? How often? Is it to contact their friends only or to promote their businesses?

Example: Men's Fitness Facebook page

Q1 – Age range is 16-35

Q2 – The potential audience is global. But is **limited to those who speak English**. Hence, primarily those who live in the US, UK, Australia, Canada.

Q3 – The gender distribution will be 80% Men, 20% Women

Q4 – They are likely to be university students or young workers. As they are very dedicated to fitness, they must have a lot of free time.

Q5 – Young people interested in fitness are likely to be very active on social media. Primary use would be for personal and social uses (for instance not business). They use it to post & share photos, tag friends, comment, etc

Facebook Analytics

Facebook is the social media platform that offers the most detailed statistics on page viewers today. In Facebook Analytics (see chapter 10), there is an entire section that provides demographic breakdown and statistics on your page audience. Using this tool you can develop a precise, statistical knowledge of your target audience. By regularly checking this tool you can see whether the target audience of your page is expanding, narrowing, reshaping, etc...

Chapter 7 – Determine what your Customers value

If you want your Facebook page to engage millions of users your content needs to be of exceptional quality, this is not up for debate. Your posts needs to be better than your competition, much better. If you want to continuously attract new users and peek their interest you must provide them with content they **value.**

Value is a word that is thrown around the marketing industry very often, albeit is generally misunderstood. From a high-level perspective it is easily defined: *your audience attributes a level of importance, worth and usefulness to your content.* However, it is extremely difficult to define *exactly* what your audience values about your content and your posts, especially in the digital media industry.

For instance cat memes are extremely popular across the web, but can you describe why people **value** or enjoy in these memes? They are not high quality pictures, they are not revolutionary, are they original? Do people enjoy these memes because they can relate to the everyday problems they portray? Do users find these memes funny because they convey a message through the personification of an unlikely and cute pet in original and unexpected ways? If you plan to launch a page about cat memes, you have to make sure you have the answer to these questions.

Determining exactly what your users/customers value is one of the most difficult aspects of the marketing industry. However, this is also the most critical task: once you discover exactly what your audience is looking for you will be able to satisfy a market need and thus attract new users, skyrocketing their level of engagement in your content.

From the previous section in the book you should have developed a fundamental understanding of your target audience. You should have developed an appreciation for features such as age range, daily lifestyle/habits, social media habits and gender distribution of your followers. Use these insights to help you understand what they value, what the market demands are and what they are searching for.

To develop an understanding of exactly what your audience values, you can follow the approach presented below:

Step 1 - Assess the competition - first draft of Market needs & value proposition

When starting off a new Facebook page, as with any business for that matter, the first approach I always recommend is assessing the competition. Earlier in the guide I described the importance of having competition, it proves there is an audience and market need for your theme on social media.

Look at small and large competitors within your field; the smaller pages are your immediate competition and the larger pages are your long-term competition.

Look at 5 small and 5 large pages in your field, for each write down:

- **3 aspects of their profile you like** (i.e. they are funny, high quality photos, they are relatable, and they show behind-the-scenes videos…)

- **3 aspects of their profile you do not like.** For each of these points write down how you might fix this problem, it does not have to be a perfect solution. It is an initial through-provoking exercise to develop your critical thinking and market analysis skills.
- **3 aspects of their profile you think the users value:** this is their value proposition. Why are users following this page? What do you think engages them? Why are they interested in their posts?

After carrying out this procedure for ten competitors, you will have developed a good understanding for the market you are in and your competition. Finally, **summarize in ten simple statements what people liked most about the profiles and how you could have improved it**. Think critically: *"why were people following these pages?"*, *"what were they trying to get out of it?"* Look at the comments on their posts, analyse the people's response and feedback. Summarizing the successful features of their content will serve as foundation for your profile's value proposition. Remember: *Steal the positives from your competition, learn from their mistakes.*

Step 2 - Refine & improve your value proposition list

During the previous step you developed a concise list describing why, in your opinion, users are attracted to your competitors. However, copying the competition has never led anyone to success, you must improve on it. You must differentiate yourself and, in order to steal *market share*, you must provide content of better value.

To accomplish this objective, you must refine the value proposition list as described below

Step 1 – Compare your value proposition to the target audience profile you developed. Can any of these aspects be optimized to the age range, habits, gender of your target audience?

Step 2 - Play to your strengths. Do you or your team possess any unique skills you can exploit? For instance, are you an excellent web developer, an outstanding Photoshop user, an incredible video editor or a wizard at mixing soundtracks? Definitely bring these factors into your page to set yourself apart from the competition and provide your audience with unique content only you can provide.

Step 3 - Produce content. Following your value proposition, which you adapted in step 2 above, produce and launch content to your new page (more information on doing this effectively in later chapters).

Step 4 - Evaluate Feedback, improve and start again. As with any new business venture in life you will encounter criticism. A large portion of people decide to blindly ignore all criticism and carry on their own path convinced they know better; this is clearly the wrong approach. You will receive a lot of feedback from your audience in the form of comments, messages and likes. You must assess a portion of this feedback and reject the remaining portion. Look for constructive criticism, focus on it and try to isolate what the users are telling you, what they like and what they would like to see. If some posts receive 1000 likes and other photos 50 likes, analyse the differences between them and critically deduce what your users are looking for.

You must try and isolate *why* your audience responds positively to some posts. Once you have an initial theory, you must test the market! Post a new photo that addresses all of the customer feedback and examine the new response. Again, you will face positive and negative feedback; examine the new feedback, evaluate where you improved and try to improve again. This is a process of *continuous improvement* and is what will ultimately lead to market domination. It is a lot of constant work, but ultimately will lead you to success.

Remember: great content is a prerequisite for a successful Facebook page, but it is only one of the many factors that must come into place perfectly. Having exceptional quality will not give you Facebook success—marketing, advertising, consistency, engaging followers, patience and more advanced strategies (discussed later) are also required.

Chapter 8- Everything about Facebook Pages

Facebook pages can be created with many different intentions and goals in mind. There is no set purpose for all pages on Facebook, their ultimate end goal is determined by the creator. Generally, users tend to like or 'engage' with Facebook pages that portray content, messages or ideals that they share. They like and follow these pages because they are searching for 'value', which may come in the form of regular updates on a topic, social events, discounts, funny memes, creative pictures... These are the main categories of Facebook pages you are likely to come across:

- Small, local business or shop: your local grocery
- Large Corporation, company or institution: ExxonMobil, Ferrari, Starbucks...
- A product or brand page: Apple MacBook Pro page, Nike Airmax page, a new coffee flavour...
- Public figure: artist, athlete, politician, activist...
- Entertainment: local cinema, local theatre
- Cause or community: helping refugees, donating charity towards the homeless...

How can a page help grow your vision

The purpose of this book is to help you grow a Facebook page, reach millions of likes and skyrocket user engagement. Once you establish a strong social media presence the images, videos, stories, posts you share can have a great impact:

- Personalize your brand amongst all the competition
- You can generate traffic towards your website, product page, affiliation pages (generate revenue)
- Educate your following and raise awareness
- Promote a movement, activity and interactions amongst your members

As mentioned earlier, the most important metric for your page is ENGAGEMENT. This is what will build brand loyalty and customer dedication. You are not aiming for high page visits, but a high engagement.

How to set up a Facebook Page

The following sections will cover how to select, develop and launch a Facebook page that reflects your social media goals. Inside Facebook, select the 'create a page' command to begin this process.

Selecting page category

The first action towards the creation of a new Facebook page is the selection of a page category, shown below. Although all pages appear similar to one another, each possesses individual features and traits that you can promote to the public.

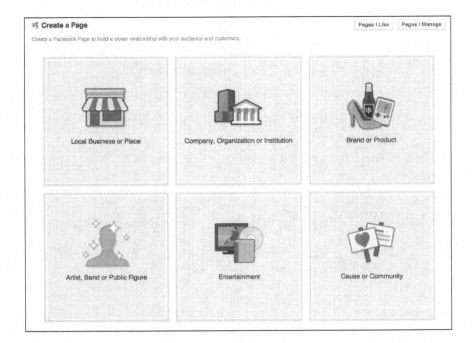

Page Basic Information

After selecting a page type, a creation wizard will appear and you will be asked to provide a set of information regarding the new page. Each page category requires a different set of information, specifically relevant to the category. After creation, you can change the page category information as often as you like without constraints. Beware that if you change the page category from "local business" page, any reviews you currently possess will be lost. Shown below is the set-up information required by every page category during setup.

Detailed Page Information

After adding the minimum requirements above, your page can go live on Facebook. However, the creation wizard will ask for additional details about your page; these provide more information to the page visitors and help you gain more exposure. Let's use the "Local Business or Place" page category as an example, this is some of the extra information you can provide:

In addition to the information above you have the ability to customize the URL address of your page, add a detailed page description, provide tags that identify your page for greater visibility when searched, and more. At this point you must also provide a page profile picture and you will be asked whether you wish to add this page to your favourites and—if there are any page duplicates for your business—you will have the opportunity to claim those pages also. Finally, Facebook will ask for a preferred audience; this provides specified demographics characteristics for your target audience. In order to publish your page you will have to certify that you possess the right and authority to represent the chosen business. At this stage, your page will be live on Facebook!

Customizing your page

In the previous sections, the guide described how to get a facebook page published. In the following sections the guide will dive into the process of customizing what is–for now—a mostly empty Facebook page. The main features and commands available in your Facebook page are also explained.

Introducing your new page

Although your page is now live and visible on facebook, it has an empty and bleak appearance. Before you start working on the appearance of the page and introduce some eye-catching graphics, it is important that you verify the information you entered is corrected; you will also be able to update any information in the future in case you choose to do so.

While on your page, you can click on the 'about' tab to verify/update the following information relating to your business:

- Address
- Contact ifnormation
- Operating Hours
- Price Range
- Link to Website URL
- And more

Add Cover photo & Display photo (profile picture)

Now, is time to add some colour and creative touch to your page by adding the cover and display photo. The display photo is a small, squared picture of size 180x180 pixels. This photo will always be displayed in each of your posts and therefore will be inextricably linked to your page. Make sure it is something catchy creative and unique to your page, which can be easily recognized. A logo is typically used for these photos, if you don't have a logo you can hire a graphic designer to create a simple logo for 5$ on Fiverr.com.

The cover photo should be something creative, unique and colourful. It should represent the message, character and style of your page. Make sure it is a photo that adds depth to your page, the dimensions are 851x315 pixels. Again, you can hire graphic designers of Fiverr.com to design a high-quality, catchy cover photo that matches the style/direction of your Facebook page.

Look at Apple's facebook page, the display photo is the logo and the background picture is a high-quality representation of their newest most succesfull product.

Adding 'Call-to-Action' buttons

Call-to-action buttons are the "Buy Now", "Book Now", "Contact Us" buttons you see on a the top of some facebook pages. These buttons are very powerful in redirecting visiors towards a very specific purpose or website. These may include buying a product, booking tickets for an event or contacting a restaurant for a takeout order. The buttons work across desktop, iphone and android users alike. There are a number of call-to-action buttons at your availability: BOOK NOW

- CALL NOW
- CONTACT US
- SEND MESSAGE
- USE APP
- PLAY GAME
- SHOP NOW
- SIGN UP
- WATCH VIDEO

The image below shows how these buttons are selected and added to your page.

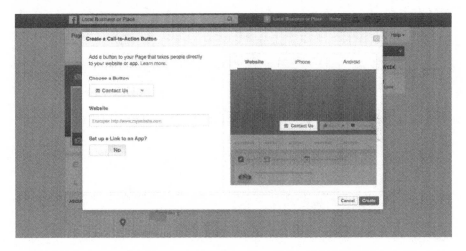

Explore the page 'Settings'

The settings tab is where you can view and modify most information relevant to your page, for instance the privacy mode of your page. You can choose user/admin roles, select page members who are not allowed to post in your page to prevent spam. Other settings you can modify here include: who can find your page, who can comment on your posts, who can tag on photos, who can privately message you (the page owner), and whether there are age or country restrictions to viewers of your page.

⚙ **General**	Favorites	Page is not added to Favorites	Edit
💬 Messaging	Page Visibility	Page published	Edit
ⓘ Page Info	Visitor Posts	Anyone can publish to the Page Anyone can add photos and videos to the Page	Edit
≈ Post Attribution	News Feed Audience and Visibility for Posts	The ability to narrow the potential audience for News Feed and limit visibility on your posts is turned off	Edit
📣 Notifications	Expiring Posts	Ability to set posts that expire is turned off for my Page	Edit
👤 Page Roles	Messages	People can contact my Page privately.	Edit
👥 People and Other Pages	Tagging Ability	Only people who help manage my Page can tag photos posted on it.	Edit
👥 Preferred Page Audience	Country Restrictions	Page is visible to everyone.	Edit
⚙ Apps	Age Restrictions	Page is shown to everyone.	Edit
📷 Instagram Ads	Page Moderation	No words are being blocked from the Page.	Edit
★ Featured	Profanity Filter	Turned off	Edit
📝 Page Support	Similar Page Suggestions	Choose whether your Page is recommended to others	Edit
	Comment Ranking	Most recent comments are shown for my Page by default.	Edit
≡ Activity Log	Merge Pages	Merge duplicate Pages	Edit
	Remove Page	Delete your Page	Edit

Chapter 9- Facebook Advertising

Ad campaigns on Facebook are a massive topic that takes years of marketing experience to perfect and understand in every detail. This book will give the readers an overview of why you need Facebook ads, how to set up the two most effective types of ad campaigns: "promote your page" and "boos post", how to specify a target audience for maximum campaign success and how to use Facebook Analytics to learn & improve future campaigns. I will also show you the details of an ad campaign I used to gain 5,000 likes for 15$; the campaign is perfectly repeatable and you will experience similar results when running it. I encourage you to run it when launching a new page in order to acquire your first 10,000 likes, hence achieve social proof for any new page visitor.

Overview of facebook ads

Over the past years facebook has directed a lot of effort towards building an effective advertising platform. In today's world, Facebook is seen as the most cost-effective and targeted framework to market a product or a service directly to the end customer. The great marketing success of Facebook is based on 3 key features: (1) Global Reach (2) Targeted Advertising (3) Instantaneous and Detailed Feedback.

1 – **Global Reach**: with facebook's 1.9 billion monthly active users, massive marketing campaigns can be launched to a truly global reach. However, one of facebook's great unique

advantages is its ability to provide small-scale marketing campaigns for all budgets.

2 – **Targeted Advertising**: with society's increasing participation in social media, through every page you like and comment you place, Facebook gains more knowledge on your preferences, interestes and activities. This data represents Facebook's strongest point in advertisement: the ability to target individual customers based on their social media activities. The ads targets can be narrowed down by age, nationality, language, interests, geographical location, and much more

3 – **Instantenous and Detailed Feedback**: It has never been this simple and straightforward to analyse the success of a marketing campaign. Extensive set of deatailed statistics are presented in Facebook Analytics (see chapter 10) detailing exactly who and what features proved most responsive during the campaign. Perhaps most useful of all, small ad campaigns can be launched to only reach a few thousand people (yes, that is small by facebook standards). By doing so, different ad strategies can be run in parallel and, using facebook analytics, the most responsive feautres of each ad strategy can be isolated before launching a large-scale ad campaign. This quick and inexpensive feedback strategy was not available with older marketing approaches—such as magazine adverts.

Creating Ads

Before you can launch your first campaign, you need to have a verified billing method for your account (required to fund the marketing campaign). Enter the billing inforamtion as required in Manage Ads>Settings>Billing.

Now that your billing information is set, you can proceed to launhc your first marketing campaign. To do this, you must select the "Create Ads" menu and navigate through the ad manager menu.

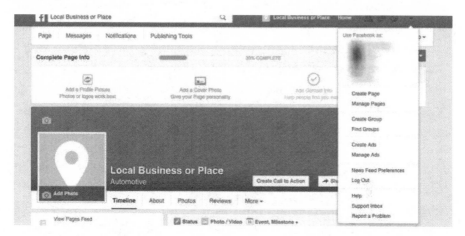

Aftwerwards you will be asked to select an objective for your ad campaign, your options are:

- **Boost your posts** (promote a single post)
- **Promote your page** (page likes)
- Send people to your website
- Increase conversions on your website
- Get installs of your app
- Increase engagement in your app
- Reach people near your business
- Raise attendance at your event
- Get people to claim your offer
- Get video views

Although each ad purpose will require different specific information, there are features common to all:

1. Naming the Ad campaign
2. Selecting a target demographic (age, location, gender, ...)
3. User interests
4. Costing of advertisement

Promote Your Page

The 'promote your page' campaing is—wihtout doubt—one of the best strategies to increase the number of likes your page gets at a very reasonable budget. Note that this marketing campaign was devised by facebook with the purpose of increaseing the number of page likes, it may only produce a small increases in user engagement. In a later section I will show you exactly how I acquired 5,000 page likes for $15 using this campaign method.

From the previous screen, select the "Manage Ads" command and the "promote your page" command as shown below. Beofre publishing your ad, you will have to select an audience, ad placement, campaign costs and other campaign features. These will be explained in later sections.

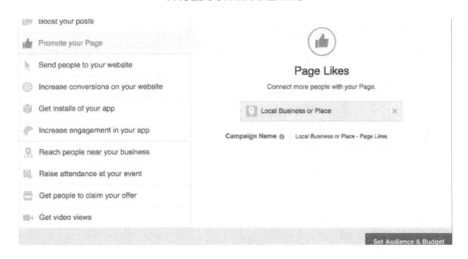

Boosting your post

Boosting your post can be very effective when releasing a particularly captivating and catchy post. This post is supposed to represent everythign your page stands for in a positive and flattering manner. This technique is aimed at increasing user **engagement**, not page likes. However, you will gain likes for the post and if it is captivating engouh, you can expect users to start tagging their friends and achieve a wider audience. In short, using this technique although you may gain few page likes, you will increase user engagement provided the audience you target finds your post very appealing.

To begin, create a first post that is captivating and eye-catching to your target audience as described above. Click the boos post button to begin the ad campaing. When you arrange for a delayed post publication time, the corresponding campaign will als be delayed.

Create a New Audience

Both of the above marketing campaigns require you to select an audience. For your first campaign you will have to create a new audience, for later campaigns you will be able to slect/edit saved audeicnes or create new ones.

In this area, you can specify the demographics of the audience you would like to reach. In chapter 6 I discussed how you can understand and define your target audience precisely; use that information to create extremetly targeted and focused ads. The screen below shows how to create and specify a new audience for your first marketign campaign.

Pro Tip: If you are only looking to increase page likes, make sure you select the "Exclude people who like [your page name]", this prevents advertising your page to those who already like it.

Facebook provides a very helpful graphical representation of the audience details, breadth, characteristics and potential reach. Estimates for daily reach are calclulated based on the campaign daily budget allocated (pricing is explained in the later section).

As you refine the audience requirements, the "potential reach" of your ad will change. This number represents the global facebook users that meet the characteristics of your audience.

If your potential reach is very large, then you can refine your audience further and ideally target more receptive customers (gauge points at "broad"). If your potential audience is too small for your campaign requirements, then your audience is too refined and you should proceed to widen your audience (gauge points at "specific"). Ideally, for your first campaigns you should maintain the gauge on the green area. It is worth mentioning that the more refined the audience, the higher the advertising costs.

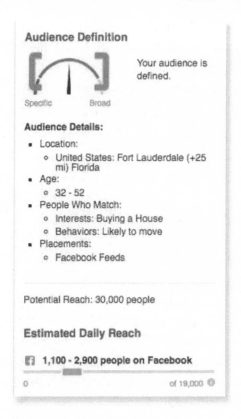

Audience Definition

Your audience is defined.

Specific   Broad

Audience Details:

- Location:
  - United States: Fort Lauderdale (+25 mi) Florida
- Age:
  - 32 - 52
- People Who Match:
  - Interests: Buying a House
  - Behaviors: Likely to move
- Placements:
  - Facebook Feeds

Potential Reach: 30,000 people

Estimated Daily Reach

 1,100 - 2,900 people on Facebook

0   of 19,000

Ad placement and pricing

In the next steps you will be required to select ad placement, budget, schedule and format. Facebook will walk you through these menus and most menu options are self-explanatory. However, I would like to point out a few lessons I have learned during past campaigns.

Placement – This option allows you to the location of your ad to the viewers. You can choose between different platforms and locations. I have experienced greatest marketing success when selecting facebook as a platform and the "Feeds" location (ads will be placed in the news feed section of your target customers).

40

Pricing – In this section you must specify budget of your campaign. Make sure you select "Automatic" for the Bid Amount option, as facebook will always deliver the cheapest bid available. This is preferential to the manual big pricing because, as your post engagement increases, the bid price will decrease also.

Test campaigns in parallel

I have already skimmed over this topic previously, but it deserves further mention due to its crucial impact on the success of any marketing campaign. When preparing any form of promotional content (radio ads, magazine ads, commercials...), it is common practice to prepare two or three versions, compare one another and pick the most responsive ad. In the past this was difficult to do: unbiased test candidates are gathered and they are exposed to the promotional content; their response is recorded and assessed.

Facebook ads make this process immensely faster, easier and more precise. Before launching a very large marketing campaign, you can set up small facebook ads of 10$ with all your different advertising strategies. Facebook can launch the ads immediately and within the next day UNBIASED, REAL-CUSTOMER responses are available.

This process is clearly fast and effecting; I ALWAYS recommend testing multiple advertising strategies in parallel over facebook before launching a large marketing campaign.

Exactly how I got 5,000 likes for $15

So far in the guide I have discussed the principles of social media marketing and how to create successful Facebook ads. However, all of the information I have presented was theoretical. You—the reader—might be wondering what kind of results I can obtain TODAY on using the techniques presented in this book.

To PRACTICALLY demonstrate you this, I have created a brand new Facebook page about emotions & love and launched a fairly broad "promote your page" campaign. The budget was 15$ and it ran over 3 days, **after 10 days my brand new page had 4,867 likes!** Keep in mind this was only a test page and I was not after user engagement. Below are reported the results of my ad campaign:

In this chapter I will show you exactly how I used the "promote your page" campaign to obtain this, using the steps and strategies from earlier in the book.

Defining the audience

Given that this was a quickly drawn-up page about love, I decided to maintain a "fairly broad" audience, as described by facebook. The few key traits in this definition are shown below.

Audience definition

Your audience
selection is fairly
broad.

Specific   Broad

Audience Details:

- Location:
  - Worldwide
- Exclude Location:
  - United States: California
- Excluded Connections:
  - Exclude people who like ████████
- Age:
  - 13-24
- Language:
  - English (All)
- People who match:
  - Interests: Love
- Placements:
  - Facebook Feeds and Facebook Right column

Potential reach: 918,000,000 people

Here is a brief explanation of how I set up the target audience:

- I decided avoided advertising in California because it is much more expensive compared to other places.
- As my page is in English, I only advetise to users whose first language is english
- Interests: love, this matches what my page is all about
- Exclude people who already like my page from seeing my ads, as I can not receive any additional likes from these users.

Pricing

As previously explained, I spent $15 on this campaign ove the course of 3 days, here is a screenshot of the Budgeting settings:

Ad Preview

The final section of the Ad is the preview section, where you can modify the text that will appear in your ad. A preview of the final ad as seen by the users is provided and is updated as you insert new information.

In this section you can modify, view and adjust the exact text that will be displayed onto the ad. The following information can be filled in as desired, this is how I have filled it in.

I selected a high-impact photogrpah without copyright, which allows free unrestriced redistribution. My favourite only source for copyright-free images is www.pixabay.com.

Below is the preview of my ad as it will appear to users. The key features are that it is a high-impact, eye-catching ad that is likely to attract the viewer's attention as he scrolls through the news feed.

Results

Here are the results I obtained from the marketing campaign.

Clearly, this campaign is extremely effective at acquiring likes for a very low budget; you can follow the steps above to launch your own campaigns to experience similar results. Even if your page is not about love you can still employ the campaign above to earn a high amount of likes for a new page, this is useful only because it gives new page visitors 'social validation'. Organic

45

growth is much more difficult for a page with 24 likes, than a page with 5,000.

I suggest using the above campaign to only earn your first 5-10,000 likes, as your user eengagement does not increase. When pages have 60,000 likes and a post has 2 comments, it is never a good sign. From a business perspective the worth of your page is purely based on user engagement, not likes.

Chapter 10- Facebook Analytics

Facebook provides an extensive set of statistics for your page, these provide critical analysis on the growth of your page, success of your marketing campaigns and levels of user engagement. This chapter will cover the most important features found in analytics section. However, the quickcest way to understand how these analytics work is by **doing**: play around with them, test them and explore all of its features section as much as you can. You must become very familiar with all the features and this is only achieved with experience. This feature is also known as **facebook insights**.

Analytics overview

When you first open the analytics, you are presented with overview information.

The above screen provides a broad overview of the page visitors, user engagement and devices used to visit your page. The toolbar on the left allows you to navigate through to different sections and access more detailed page statistics.

"Likes"

In the likes sub-section, the total amount of page likes is displayed. You will have the ability how track how page likes have changed over the past 30 days as well as variations in **Net Likes**, meaning how many new likes you have earned every day.

Another important statistic presented is the origin of your page like. That is, how did users who liked your page find it? Did they land on your page through ads, direct link, API, etc... This is really helpful in understanding how your page is growing and how it is impacting people.

"Reach"

Reach represents the amount of users that have seen your post. Facebook provides a very useful graph that differentiates between organic reach and paid reach. Again, you can use this to understand how your page is growing and how it is affecting people. This is shown in the figure below.

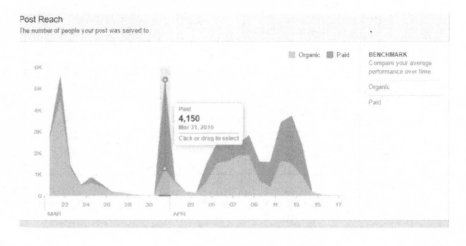

48

Paid marketing campaigns (targetting user engagement) will produce a very sharp spike in paid engagement and slight spike inorganic reach, after the campaign is finished paid engagement will fade away and organic engagement will take a dip. If the campaign was succesfull, you should see organic engagement began a steady increase afterwards.

"Page Views"

This section allows you to see how many people are viewing your page over time. I personally really like this for understanding my conversion rate. That is, how does my post engagement compare to page views? For instance if a post has a reach of 100 users and I receive 5 page views, than that is a conversion rate of 5% (8% is usually a good target and 12-15% is extremely good). This type of analytics works particularly well with a new pages. Similarly, you can calculate the conversion rate of page views to new page likes, although you must account for users who have already liked your page. Take a look below at the graphical representation facebook offers:

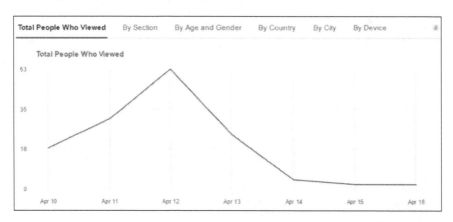

Although there is no means of differing between organic and paid page views, there is a number of audience refinement you can carrry out:

- Total Page Views
- Views by section
- Views by age & gender
- Views by country
- Views by city
- Views by device (laptop, mobile, ...)

"Actions on page"

This section shows what activity users engage in while visiting your page. Facebook provides statistics for how many users are engaging/clicking on the following actitivites:

- Directions
- Phone numbers
- Website clicks
- Call-to-action buttons

(audience can be refined according to section, age, gender, country, city, device)

"Posts"

In this section you can see a list of all your past posts. For each post, facebook will tell you how much engagement and reach it received. You have the option to boost posts and examine the results of "boost your post" campaigns. The demographic for all of these options can be assess and examined.

There is also a useful section describing when when your audience was online and active on facebook; information is presented both daily and hourly. This statistics is useful in planning out your posting times and schedule, as shown below.

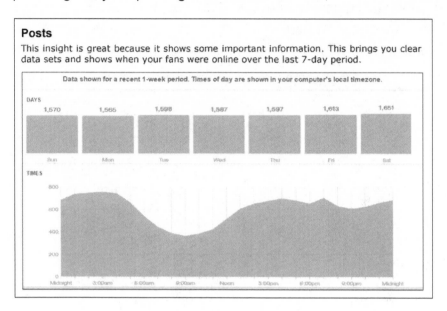

"Videos"

This menu offers functionality and analysis that is very similar to the Posts subsection, only that it targets videos. You can examine the reach and engagement of your videos and assess the target demographic.

"People"

This is arguably one of the most important sections in facebook analytics. It helps you understand the demographic of the audience you reached, engaged and who your fans are. I discussed the importance of understanding your target audience earlier in the guide, well here facebook does most of the work for you!

By understanding who best responds to your page, you can more precisely define an audience for any future marketing campaigns you launch. Here is a screen of the inforamtion facebook offers the users in this section.

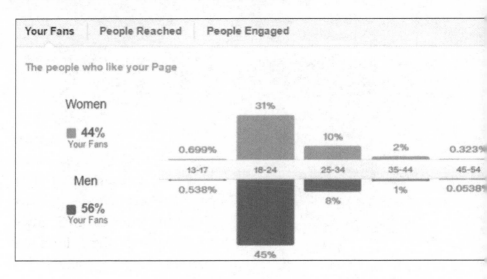

Chapter 11 – Develop Content Strategy

In this chapter, the book will discuss how you can deliver valued content effectively and consistently your Facebook users.

Establishing content Guidelines for your page (consider outsourcing)

As you first develop a Facebook page it is recommended to remain spontaneous and varied in the types of post you deliver (remaining within your value proposition guidelines). However, as your brand expands you should consider establishing style templates for your content. These should summarize key features that define the quality and style of your content. Style templates can define many features of your content, from the hashtags you use to the colour schemes of your pictures. In short, style template provide a set of guidelines that a piece of content must follow. Subjects they could cover are:

- Hashtags
- Brand Aesthetics
- Composition
- Colour patterns
- Subjects
- Background
- Length of text
-

If your page has developed a very large following or you are now trying to grow multiple Facebook pages, these guidelines ensure you do not lose brand image. Furthermore, if you consider outsourcing the creation of content (as most large businesses do) a style template ensures the third party designer produces content that matches your brand image.

With a clearly-defined content guideline, outsourcers can take over the majority of the day-to-day tasks required by a large Facebook account, while you keep the revenue it provides. Freelancers can be found easily on the web with excellent skills and due to geographical location they have very low hourly work rate, ex: 4$/hr. My favourite websites are upwork.com and fiverr.com.

Define Content type and ratios

Facebook was originally developed to bring text, but over the year it has developed much further; it now supports a wide variety of content, from videos and vines to the more recently Facebook stories. Producing different types of content is a great strategy to attract new users and increase the engagement levels of page followers. Define a ratio of alternating content and try to stick with it, for example "I will post one video every 20 images".

Determine a posting frequency

When you initially start your page, a low posting frequency is recommended (less than one post a day). However as your page scales and you begin to develop a following, it is recommended to post more than once a day. A well-defined posting frequency is required for a high user engagement and 'customer loyalty', users will regularly visit your page expecting a new posts, do not disappoint!

Posting Schedule

It is usually a good idea to write down your posting pattern. It will help maintaining regular posting frequency and content delivery. Here is an example of an intensive posting schedule for a medium-sized Facebook page (100k likes):

Day	Morning	Afternoon
Monday	Written Post – update on new week	Photo
Tuesday	Video	/
Wednesday	Photo	Photo
Thursday	Photo	Written post
Friday	Photo	Written post- end of week
Saturday	Photo	video
Sunday	Q&A from audience	/

Consider user-generated content

For pages with an active following, sharing user-generated content can be an excellent strategy to increase engagement. Although curating all the user-generated content can impose a significant toll in terms of time and effort, the benefits are worth it. It is an incentive for users to creatively interact with your own products, images and really feel part of the brand. The effort they dedicate towards creating content solidifies their bond with your page. In the future they will become more active and more inclined to share your page with their friends. When sharing user-content, be sure to tag the creator.

Chapter 12- Guide to outsourcing your Facebook page

As already mentioned earlier in the guide, you should outsource the daily activities of a facebook page as early as possible. Many fear that outsourcing is expensive and will lead to a decrease in content quality. In this guide I will show you why this is not true, ad how to begin outsourcing your activities.

Benefits of outsourcing

When dealing with social media there are many repetitive tasks that require continuous attention, for instance posting photos or replying to comments. Many of these tasks require a fast response to the customer to ensure maximum growth and engagement.

It is important to minimize your involvement in daily page maintenance/operations for a number of reasons. You gain more time to focus on the strategic development of the page, such as targeting new audiences, launching new marketing campaigns or researching new content. You reduce your daily commitments to the page, which means if you get sick the entire operation does not crash. Most importantly, it provides extra free time to pursue new activities in your life. This means you can create more facebook pages, new business ventures or activities of any sort.

In short, outsourcing removes you from the daily running of the page, which makes this **SCALEABLE.**

Build a revenue from your page

I am a strong believer that any facebook page should be self-sustaining, both in terms of daily operations management and monetary investment. Achieving this goal requires your page to start generating an income. Monetizing a Facebook page may seem impossible to those with little experience in digital marketing, but in today's world as long as you have an audience you can easily earn money. However, you must be careful in choosing HOW you will monetize your page as, you do not want to become perceived as a 'sell-out' by your users, which reduces their brand loyalty.

I have provided the link to a free guide on monetizing your facebook page below, it covers in detail all the different strategies and concerns associated with monetizing your first Facebook page. It is important to start monetizing your page as early as possible and scale the income streams as your page scales.

For a free guide explaining how you can monetize your first Facebook page visit:

www.bit.ly/facebookpageincome

What tasks can you outsource?

Outsourcing your page is a critial part of scaleability, but for those with lesser experience in social media marketing a very gradual approach should be employed. You should only outsource tasks you have mastered and can be carried out under a strict set of guidelines without your personal supervision.

Examples of facebook marketing tasks to outsource:

- Research, Design and Posting of new content – refer to content strategy in chapter 11
- Responding to user comments and Direct Messages
- Create monthly reports on analytics (ad campaign, growth, engagement, likes, …)
- Researching & assessing your competition
- Contacting other Facebook pages for collaborations/cross-promotion

Managing a Virtual Assistant

For those who have never worked with virtual assistants, there are afew things that must be noted.

Giving instrcuctions- Your aim is to provide the minimum amount of information for a VA to complete a task without having to contact you again. You must be very clear and detailed, but not write excessively detailed instructions or it will take too much time. After reading the instructions, your VA should feel "*I know exactly what I have to do and how to do it*".

It is also important to plan for accidents and unexpected events using an "**if, then**" approach. For instance if one of the comments of your page is offensive, then he should not respond but rather remove it. Finally, remember that VAs have previous experience in social media marketing and are quite well-versed in this field. Give them some freedom to manouvre and take the initiative, for instance "if [this scenario happens], resort to best judgement".

Set an hourly/budget limit- This is something that did not occur to me when I first hired a VA and proved a very expensive mistake. Make sure that whenever you assign a task to your VA, you clearly state a budget or hourly limit.

Where to Find Virtual Assistants

Virtual Assistants can be found easily on the web with excellent skills and due to geographical locations they can work for very low hourly work rate, ex: 4$/hr. My favourite resources for hiring Virtual Assistants are: upwork.com, Fiverr.com or freelance.com.

When hiring a virtual assistant you should advertise a job posting requiring the applicants answer a set of questions (ex. describing their past experiences in social media marketing). Based on the answers provided, you can select the most thorough/committed applicants. For very large tasks I recommend a Skype interview/discussion with a few shortlisted candidates before hiring.

Example of outsourcing a Facebook Page

This is an example of posts made by a virtual assistant for a Facebook page about sneakers. Instructions were given to find trendy pictures of sneakers on a clear background, place their name and source in the ribbon and put the page logo in the bottom right corner. The virtual assistant proceeded to post them on the facebook page every other day. This is some of the content he created. As a page grows in following and higher quality is desired, assistants with greater abilities in graphic design can be hired.

Conclusion

Thank you for reading this book, I hope you found it helpful!

In this guide, I have explained the main strategies and techniques I have used to successfully grow various Facebook pages to over 1 million likes. I have placed a strong importance on technical terminology such as target audience, value proposition and market demand. Even though many of you may never have thought about these aspects, these are critical to your future success as a digital marketer.

In have provided a step-by-step blueprint I personally use to grow new Facebook pages to the threshold of 1 million followers. Follow this guide as closely as you can, but never forget the key to entrepreneurial success: hard work and continuous improvement!

Thank you for reading,

Pamela Russell

DO YOU WANT TO LEARN MORE ABOUT DIGITAL MARKETING AND INSTAGRAM?

CHECK OUT MY AMAZON BESTSELLER!

AVAILABLE ON AMAZON TODAY!

Made in the USA
San Bernardino, CA
09 August 2017